Assessing the Progress of New American Schools

A Status Report

Mark Berends

with
Joanna Heilbrunn
Christopher J. McKelvey
Thomas Sullivan

Prepared for
New American Schools

RAND
EDUCATION

The research described in this report was supported by New American Schools.

Library of Congress Cataloging-in-Publication Data

Berends, Mark, 1962-
    Assessing the progress of New American Schools : a status report / Mark Berends with Joanna Heilbrunn, Christopher McKelvey, Thomas Sullivan.
        p.   cm.
    "MR-1085-EDU."
    Includes bibliographical references (p).
    ISBN 0-8330-2761-1
    1. New American Schools (Organization).   2. School improvement programs—United States—Evaluation.
    3. Educational change—United States.   I. Title.
    LB2822.82.B45   1999
    371.2 ' 00973—dc21   99-44907
                                                                      CIP

Building on more than 25 years of research and evaluation work, RAND Education has as its mission the improvement of educational policy and practice in formal and informal settings from early childhood on. RAND is a nonprofit institution that helps improve policy and decisionmaking through research and analysis. RAND® is a registered trademark. RAND's publications do not necessarily reflect the opinions or policies of its research sponsors.

Published 1999 by RAND
1700 Main Street, P.O. Box 2138, Santa Monica, CA 90407-2138
1333 H St., N.W., Washington, D.C. 20005-4707
RAND URL: http://www.rand.org/
To order RAND documents or to obtain additional information, contact Distribution Services: Telephone: (310) 451-7002; Fax: (310) 451-6915; Internet: order@rand.org

As a private nonprofit corporation, New American Schools (NAS) began in 1991 to fund the development of designs aimed at transforming entire schools at the elementary and secondary levels. Having completed its competition, development, and demonstration phases, NAS currently is scaling-up its designs to form a critical mass of schools within several partnering districts.

The purpose of this report is to describe the baseline characteristics, such as school demographics and performance, of a large number of NAS sites in the early implementation stages of NAS's scale-up phase. During this phase, RAND's research activities include monitoring the progress of a large sample of NAS schools in eight jurisdictions from the 1994–1995 school year through the 1999–2000 school year. This report provides a description of the schools' demographics, climate, and test scores. The next step in the RAND analysis is to report on trends in implementation, school performance, and related factors.

RAND will monitor changes in this sample of schools over the next several years. This report establishes a baseline for tracking the changes. The hope is that all those interested in school improvement—parents, teachers, administrators, policymakers, researchers, community members, etc.—will benefit from the analysis.

Other RAND reports about New American Schools include

- *Lessons from New American Schools' Scale-Up Phase: Prospects for Bringing Designs to Multiple Schools,* Susan J. Bodily, 1998 (MR-1777-NAS).

- *New American Schools After Six Years,* Thomas K. Glennan, Jr., 1998 (MR-945-NASDC).

- *Lessons from New American Schools Development Corporation's Demonstration Phase,* Susan J. Bodilly, 1996 (MR-729-NASDC).

- *Reforming and Conforming: NASDC Principals Discuss School Accountability Systems,* Karen Mitchell, 1996 (MR-716-NASDC).

- *Designing New American Schools: Baseline Observations on Nine Design Teams,* Susan J. Bodilly, Susanna Purnell, Kimberly Ramsey, and Christina Smith, 1995 (MR-598-NASDC).

Funding for this research was provided under a contract with NAS and was supported by The Ford Foundation, The Pew Charitable Trusts, the John D. and Catherine T. MacArthur Foundation, the John S. and James L. Knight Foundation, and another donor. This report was written under the aegis of RAND Education, which is directed by Dominic Brewer (see http://www.rand.org/centers/education).

CONTENTS

Preface   iii

Figures   vii

Tables   ix

Summary   xi

Acknowledgments   xvii

Chapter One
INTRODUCTION AND RESEARCH QUESTIONS   1
The New American Schools Reform Effort   2
Key Questions Underlying RAND's Assessment   3
Organization of the Report   4

Chapter Two
TOWARD AN UNDERSTANDING OF SCHOOLWIDE
REFORMS: ASSESSMENT OF THE SCALE-UP PHASE . . .   5
Key Elements of the Designs   5
New American Schools Approach   8
Design-Based Assistance   8
Engaging District Support   9
RAND's Assessment   11
Data Collection Efforts   11
Analytic Approach to Key Questions   14
Significant Features of RAND Research   19

Chapter Three
BASELINE DESCRIPTION OF NEW AMERICAN
SCHOOLS   21

Sample of New American Schools   21
Sources of Data   23
Response Rates   23
Demographic Characteristics of Schools   24
School Climate: NAS Schools Compared to the Nation's
    Schools   27
  Problems Related to Diverse Student Populations   28
  Problems Related to Engagement of Students and
      Faculty   29
School Achievement Before Design Implementation   31

Chapter Four
    SUMMARY OF FINDINGS AND WORK AHEAD   35

References   37

1.1. Phases of New American Schools Initiative and RAND Roles 3

3.1. Percentage of Poor Students in NAS Schools, 1994–1995 25

3.2. Percentage of Racial-Ethnic Minority Students in NAS Schools, 1994–1995 26

3.3. Percentage of Elementary School Principals Reporting Moderate to Serious Problems Related to Diverse Student Populations 28

3.4. Percentage of Secondary School Principals Reporting Moderate to Serious Problems Related to Diverse Student Populations 29

3.5. Percentage of Elementary School Principals Reporting Moderate to Serious Problems Related to Engagement 30

3.6. Percentage of Secondary School Principals Reporting Moderate to Serious Problems Related to Engagement 31

3.7. Baseline Achievement Levels of NAS Sites Compared to District or State Averages on Standardized Tests 32

TABLES

2.1. Key Questions of RAND Assessment and Data
Collection Activities 15
3.1. 1995–1996 Target Sample for RAND Longitudinal
Sample 23
3.2. Principal Interview Sample, Spring 1997 24

Upon its founding in 1991, New American Schools (NAS) sought to engage the nation's best educators, business people, and researchers in the task of creating, testing, and fostering the implementation of schoolwide designs not constrained by existing regulations, rules, and conventions. These beginnings of "break the mold" schools evolved to the point where, in 1995, NAS began to widely diffuse the designs to a large number of schools within partnering school districts—a period known as its scale-up phase. NAS's mission during this phase has been to use design-based assistance to help schools and districts raise the achievement of large numbers of students.

Initially, RAND helped NAS design a request for proposals and conduct a national competition for designs. Subsequently, RAND studied the initial implementation of the designs during the development and demonstration phases, providing feedback to both NAS and the design teams. With the beginning of scale-up of the NAS designs in the fall of 1995, RAND's research agenda expanded to provide a comprehensive assessment that aims to inform NAS, the design teams, partnering jurisdictions, educators, and the general public with lessons learned about comprehensive school reform

RAND'S ASSESSMENT OF NEW AMERICAN SCHOOLS

NAS's approach is ambitious and complex. The strategy relies on school designs and design-based assistance to change the school organization, the professional life of teachers, and classroom environments as a way to improve student learning opportunities and achievement. A variety of institutional, social, political, and economic factors need to be aligned for successful implementation, consistency and coherence, and ultimate success. As a result, any assessment of the NAS initiative has to be multidimensional and multifaceted and must rely on a variety of data and a wide array of indicators. It is a difficult and analytically complex undertaking. Yet it is critical to understanding the progress of schools implementing schoolwide reform, especially because so little research has been conducted in this relatively new educational policy area.

Critical Issues

The NAS design teams and the assistance they provide aim to promote greater cohesiveness and coherence in a school's mission and programs as well as collaboration among its staff. One hypothesis is that over time, implementation within each school will deepen and all school staff will embrace and engage in activities supportive of the visions of the design, especially if the design continues to provide assistance and teachers continue to become more familiar with it. Each design may then become schoolwide, and a second hypothesis can be examined: schoolwide designs will improve teachers' and students' educational opportunities and performance.

However, a danger in educational reform initiatives—especially those within urban settings with complex economic, political, and social challenges—is that designs may be just another "program" that is turned on and off at selected times during the school day, week, and/or year. As time goes on, the NAS designs may be at risk of being turned off altogether, especially if districts and schools lose their focus on NAS and turn to other reform efforts.

This issue is one that RAND will address with its longitudinal sample of implementing NAS schools. If teachers, design teams, and districts can sustain their focus on the NAS designs to structure the educational opportunities of students and teachers, the designs will likely become more widespread within schools.

In future analyses we will examine trends in implementation to understand the degree to which key design team features become integral components of the schools in our sample. In addition, we will report trends in school performance indicators as provided by districts in their public reports about the schools' test score performance, absenteeism rates, and disciplinary problems. Most important, we will seek explanations for school performance trends within the participating school districts. Such explanations are critical for drawing lessons as the nation moves farther along the path of comprehensive school reform and considers it as a productive way to spend federal and local funds.

Key Questions

To assess this complex effort, we are conducting analyses aimed at answering five key questions:

- What were the NAS schools like before they implemented the designs?

- How have the designs and the assistance they provide evolved over time?

- Are the critical components of the NAS designs being implemented across a wide array of schools? Why or why not?

- Do the NAS designs extend beyond changes in school organization and governance and permeate classrooms to change curriculum and instruction?

- Over time, what is the progress of the schools being assisted by NAS design teams in improving student and school performance?

Data Collection

RAND is using a variety of data to address the key questions. Along with the district-provided data, we have collected information through interviews with principals and teachers, focus groups, case studies, surveys, observations, school and classroom artifacts, and document analysis. In a supplementary study of classroom practices, we are administering a commercial test to elementary students in NAS and non-NAS schools in San Antonio, Texas. All of these data inform our understanding of the reform that NAS is attempting to accomplish in districts, schools, classrooms, and the academic life of the nation's students.

PURPOSE OF THIS REPORT

This report has a dual purpose. First, it presents our data collection plan for addressing the key questions. The plan is discussed within the context of the overall NAS effort. Second, it presents our findings from answering the first question: What were the NAS schools like before they implemented the designs? We rely on data from partnering school districts and retrospective accounts provided by principals during phone interviews conducted in the spring of 1997. These data provide information about schools' demographic, climate, and performance characteristics at the beginning of NAS's scale-up phase.

SUMMARY OF FINDINGS AND FUTURE WORK

For the most part, NAS design teams began assisting schools facing many academic and social challenges. The majority of the NAS schools are urban, low-achieving, poor, and predominantly minority. Baseline information from the 1994–1995 school year reveals that NAS schools, on average, were performing at or below the district average on the mandated tests the year before designs began assisting schools in their restructuring efforts. Generally, then, NAS designs are attempting to change the academic lives of students and the professional lives of teachers in difficult environments.

NAS design teams partnered with schools that had challenging climates. We compared the NAS school climate indicators to a national sample. A greater percentage of NAS principals reported problems— including poverty, difficulties with the English language, racial-ethnic tension, lack of school readiness, student and teacher absenteeism, and verbal abuse and disrespect of teachers—than did principals in the national sample.

Whether design teams and the assistance they provide to these schools improve students' educational opportunities and performance is an open question. Future RAND reports will document and explain trends in both implementation and school performance, and the social and organizational factors related to them. The aim of our analysis is to monitor the implementation and performance trends in a large sample of NAS schools and to explain why those trends occur. With such knowledge, we will provide some additional lessons learned about the conditions under which designs can work effectively to improve student achievement across the nation.

ACKNOWLEDGMENTS

A research project such as this is never accomplished without the collaboration and cooperation of many people and organizations. We would like to thank New American Schools (NAS), The Ford Foundation, The Pew Charitable Trusts, the John D. and Catherine T. MacArthur Foundation, the John S. and James L. Knight Foundation, and another donor for their support of our research. We are also grateful to the teachers and principals in the schools who gave of their time to respond to our questions, the staff in districts and states who helped us piece together relevant data, and the design teams who clarified issues along the way. All played a crucial role in providing information we needed to better understand what kinds of schools the NAS designs are working with, and we appreciate their efforts and their dedication to improving the capacity of schools, the professional development of teachers, and the well-being of students.

We are thankful to the members of the Research Advisory Panel (funded by The Annenberg Foundation) who provide critical guidance to RAND's research on NAS: Barbara Cervone, Paul Hill, Janice Petrovich, Andrew Porter, Karen Sheingold, and Carol Weiss. We continue to learn from their experience, expertise, and encouragement. In addition, we are grateful to Tom Corcoran and Fred Newmann for sharing their expertise during the development of our principal and teacher surveys. Several colleagues within RAND also contributed to the research underlying this report, particularly Susan Bodilly, Thomas Glennan, and Sheila Kirby, all of whom provided helpful guidance, advice, and comments. We also thank Dave Adamson for his useful editorial comments, and we are indebted to

Michael Timpane of RAND and Adam Gamoran of the University of Wisconsin-Madison for their insightful reviews and useful suggestions for improving this report. The reviews of the NAS staff also contributed to changes in this document. Despite the cooperation, support, and guidance of these individuals and agencies, however, there may be errors in this report, all of which are our responsibility.

Chapter One

INTRODUCTION AND RESEARCH QUESTIONS

For some time, there have been many debates about the need to reorganize schools to create learning opportunities more consistent with the changing needs of American society. Concerns about how well the American education system is serving societal needs have a long history in this nation (Kliebard, 1986; Cuban, 1990; Tyack and Cuban, 1995). For example, the 1983 National Commission on Excellence in Education's report, *A Nation at Risk,* stated, "Our once unchallenged preeminence in commerce, industry, science, and technological innovation is being taken over by competitors throughout the world. . . . If an unfriendly power had attempted to impose on America the mediocre educational performance that exists today, we might have viewed it as an act of war." Not surprisingly, new educational interventions and experiments emerged.

The debates about the state of education in the United States will continue. And given that the recent release of the Third International Mathematics and Science Study (TIMSS) showed that U.S. high school students continue to lag behind those of other countries, efforts to improve student achievement scores in this country will also continue. In addition, as educational and income inequalities persist and American society becomes increasingly diverse, attention to equity will continue as well (see Kozol, 1991; Jencks and Peterson, 1991; Smith, 1995; National Research Council, 1997; Jencks and Phillips, 1998).

The emerging reports on the condition of American education and new policies and innovative activities have established a positive climate for reform. The conventional wisdom is that schools should and could do a better job of helping students learn basic and higher-order skills in reading, writing, mathematics, science, and technology (Newmann and Associates, 1996; Johnson and Immerwahr, 1994).

THE NEW AMERICAN SCHOOLS REFORM EFFORT

In this context, with attention directed toward improving equity and excellence, the New American Schools (NAS) initiative was launched during the summer of 1991. National educational goals emerged from policy forums such as the 1989 meeting of then President George Bush and state governors. These goals evolved into part of President Bush's *America 2000* effort to support new elementary and secondary school designs; further support for NAS was then provided through the Clinton administration's *Goals 2000*.

Despite this general federal support, NAS and the development of the designs were initially funded solely by the private sector. NAS sought to engage the nation's best educators, business people, and researchers in the task of creating, testing, and fostering the implementation of schoolwide designs not constrained by existing regulations, work rules, and conventions. Thus, NAS's aim was to help develop "break the mold" schools to provide innovative options within the public education sector as a way to better educate students for the societal needs of the 21st century.

The initial goal of NAS was to help a large number of schools change their organization and practices so as to improve student learning. To make this goal a reality, NAS organized its work into several phases:[1]

- A competition phase to solicit proposals and select designs;

- A development phase of one year to develop the ideas in the proposals in concrete ways;

---

[1]A more detailed description of the history of the NAS initiative and the design teams appears in Bodily, 1998; Glennan, 1998; and Stringfield, Ross, and Smith, 1996. See also Herman, 1999; Ball et al., 1998; Stringfield and Datnow, 1998; Datnow and Stringfield, 1997; Ross et al., 1997, 1998; and Stringfield, Millsap, and Herman, 1997. For descriptions of NAS and the design teams on the Web, see http://www.naschools.org, which has links to each design team's Web site.

- A demonstration phase of two years to pilot the designs in real school settings; and

- A scale-up phase in which the designs would be widely diffused in partnering jurisdictions across the nation.

RAND first helped NAS to design a request for proposals (RFP) and conduct a national competition for design proposals. Subsequently, RAND studied the initial implementation of the designs during the development and demonstration phases, providing feedback to both NAS and the design teams (Bodilly et al., 1995; Bodilly, 1996; Mitchell, 1996). Figure 1.1 shows the NAS phases and RAND's roles.

KEY QUESTIONS UNDERLYING RAND'S ASSESSMENT

With the beginning of scale-up of the NAS designs in the fall of 1995, RAND's research agenda expanded. We began to address broader questions to document the progress of the NAS initiative:

- What were student performance and school climate like in the NAS schools before they implemented the designs?

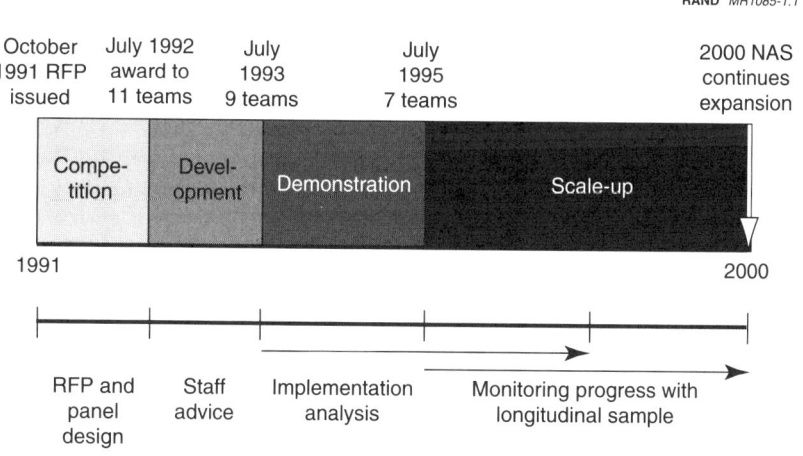

Figure 1.1—Phases of New American Schools Initiative and RAND Roles

- How have the designs and the assistance they provide evolved over time?

- Are the critical components of the NAS designs being implemented across a wide array of schools? Why or why not?

- Do the NAS designs extend beyond changes in school organization and governance and permeate classrooms to change curriculum and instruction?

- Over time, what is the progress of the schools being assisted by NAS design teams in improving student and school performance?

This report lays out RAND's analytic plan for addressing these questions. It also provides an answer to the first question: What were the NAS schools like before they implemented the designs? For this report, we rely on data from partnering school districts and retrospective accounts provided by principals during phone interviews conducted in the spring of 1997. These data provide information about the schools' demographic, climate, and performance characteristics at the beginning of NAS's scale-up phase.

ORGANIZATION OF THE REPORT

Chapter Two describes NAS's approach to schoolwide reform and RAND's overall analysis plan and data collection efforts for assessing the NAS initiative in terms of the five key questions listed above. We discuss the importance of a more thorough empirical understanding of schoolwide reforms or comprehensive school reform as the nation continues to grapple with how to improve the learning opportunities of its students. Chapter Three provides details of the RAND sample and presents a baseline description of the NAS schools in our sample in terms of their demographic and school climate characteristics. We also summarize school achievement levels during the baseline year to provide a better understanding of what the NAS schools were like before the design teams began assisting them. A brief summary of our findings and the work ahead appears in Chapter Four.

Chapter Two

TOWARD AN UNDERSTANDING OF SCHOOLWIDE REFORMS: ASSESSMENT OF THE SCALE-UP PHASE

The goal of NAS is to improve student learning. To make this goal a reality, NAS organized its work into several phases: a call for "break the mold" proposals for school designs, development and pilot implementation of those proposals, and a diffusing of the developed designs to a large number of schools within partnering school districts (NAS's scale-up phase). (For more information about the evolution of NAS, see Bodilly et al., 1995; Bodilly, 1998; Glennan, 1998.)

While private sponsorship of school innovation is not new historically (Tyack and Cuban, 1995), the NAS initiative is significant because of its focus on establishing partnerships among school designs, districts, and schools. NAS views such partnerships as key to helping a large number of schools change their organization and practices so as to improve student achievement.

KEY ELEMENTS OF THE DESIGNS

In September 1995, NAS and its partners began to bring the designs to scale—that is, to implement designs more widely within partnering districts. As NAS entered the scale-up phase, there were seven design teams:[1]

---

[1]Another design, Urban Learning Centers (ULC), was implementing in the Los Angeles area. This design team was not included in the NAS portfolio when scale-up began because it had not shown the capacity to go to scale. It since has shown this capacity and is now being marketed by NAS as one of its designs.

- Audrey Cohen College (AC) (recently renamed Purpose-Centered Education);

- Authentic Teaching, Learning, and Assessment for All Students (ATLAS);

- Co-NECT Schools (CON);

- Expeditionary Learning Outward Bound (ELOB);

- Modern Red Schoolhouse (MR);

- National Alliance for Restructuring Education (NARE) (recently renamed America's Choice Design Network); and

- Roots and Wings (RW).

Each design has unique features,[2] yet all tend to emphasize school change in the following areas:

- Organization and governance;

- Professional life of teachers;

- Content and performance expectations;

- Curriculum and instructional strategies; and

- Parent and community involvement.

The area of organization and governance refers to the authority relations among the various parties in the school. An example of a change in a governance arrangement is a reorganization of the decisionmaking processes for budgets and staffing to include teachers and other school employees and parents. Giving authority to the school site has received a great deal of attention in the education community. According to Murphy (1991), the central focus on governance restructuring stems from a belief that change must reside with those who are closest to the learners (see also Bryk et al., 1998). NAS and many of the designs strongly share this belief.

The professional life of teachers refers to the roles that teachers play and the relationships in which they participate during the school

---

[2]Currently, RAND is documenting the continued development and adaptation of the designs over time—from the initial development of the designs' educational ideas during NAS's RFP phase, through the phases in which these ideas met the economic, sociological, and political realities of implementation in schools.

day. In effect, when referring to restructuring schools, particularly those in poor, urban areas, what is involved here is overhauling the conditions under which teachers work by changing their responsibilities and tasks and by developing a more professional culture in schools (Newmann and Associates, 1996; Murphy, 1991; Sykes, 1990; Wise, 1989). In contrast to an environment in which teachers work in isolation without contact with their colleagues (Lortie, 1970), design teams aim to build a collaborative environment for teachers. Thus, it is important to understand the extent to which teachers collaborate, engaging together in activities such as professional development, common planning time, and critiquing each other's instruction. Moreover, it is important to understand the professional development activities of teachers and how these relate to changes in classroom activities.

Each of the designs aims to bring all students to high standards, even though each may use different means to attain this goal. To monitor whether designs are making progress toward this end, critical indicators might include the degree to which student assessments are explicitly linked to academic standards, teachers make performance expectations explicit to students, and the curriculum and performance standards are consistent and coherent across grade levels.

Most of the designs are concerned with shaping student experiences within classrooms to further academic achievement growth. NAS designs embrace alternative instructional strategies that involve different relationships between teachers and students and between students and subject matter. Yet, again, each design differs somewhat in the specific nature of these activities. Conventional classrooms are often characterized as "teachers talk at students and fill their heads with knowledge," and "students respond with the correct answers at appropriate times" (see Gamoran et al., 1995; Sizer, 1984; Powell, Farrar, and Cohen, 1985). In contrast, design teams tend to emphasize alternative instructional practices, such as students working in small groups, using manipulatives, engaging in student-led discussions, and working on group and/or individual projects that span a long period of time (e.g., a marking period or semester).

Closely related to instructional strategies are school decisions about how students are grouped for instruction. The effects of ability grouping and "tracking" on student achievement are strongly debated among educators and researchers (see Slavin, 1987, 1990; Gamoran and Berends, 1987; Oakes, Gamoran, and Page, 1992; Hallinan, 1994; Oakes, 1994). Yet most agree that alternatives to inflexible grouping arrangements are worth further exploration. Thus, the NAS designs have experimented with such alternative student groupings. For example, students within an ELOB or CON design may have the same teacher for several years. RW emphasizes flexibility by grouping students by achievement level in reading for part of the day and mixing students of various achievement levels for other subjects. Students are assessed every eight weeks or so to see if they would be better served by being placed in a different group. In short, each of the designs is sensitive to the issue of ability grouping and is working with schools to group students in more-effective ways.

Conventional wisdom suggests that the parent-child relationship and parent involvement in the child's education are critical components of school success. The NAS designs have embraced this issue as well. Several of them (e.g., ATLAS and RW) aim to have individuals or teams within the schools that serve as resources to students and families to help integrate the provision of social services. Others (e.g., AC, ELOB, and NARE) emphasize the need for students to apply their learning in ways that directly benefit the community. Each design desires that parents and community members be involved in positive ways in the educational program.

NEW AMERICAN SCHOOLS APPROACH

Design-Based Assistance

Because NAS believes that most schools have benefited from focused, strategic assistance in their efforts to implement a design, it now considers the support and development of design-based assistance organizations to be its most important accomplishment.[3]

---

[3]To a certain extent, this approach to supporting the diffusion of designs and design-based assistance can be characterized as NAS's "theory of action" (Weiss, 1972, 1995, 1997). Weiss's conceptualization grounds educational research and evaluation in program theories of change to articulate the explicit or implicit theories about how and why programs will work. Weiss (1995, p. 69) states four major reasons why it is useful to ground educational research and evaluation of educational programs on the theories of change underlying educational programs: (1) such research concentrates

NAS's approach to schoolwide reform relies on such design-based assistance "as its cornerstone" (Glennan, 1998, p. 14). In fact, NAS's current mission is to improve student achievement for large numbers of students through design-based assistance (New American Schools Development Corporation, 1999).

A critical aspect of design-based assistance is the designs' commitment to providing ongoing assistance to support services aimed at furthering implementation and school transformation—organization, curriculum, instruction, and professional development of staff. That is, when guided by a design and assisted by an external agent (the design team), schoolwide reform will promote greater program cohesiveness and coherence within the school, as well as collaboration among the school's staff. Such an approach will lead to school-based programs that better serve the needs of students and result in improved academic outcomes.

Toward this end, teachers and other staff in schools need to have a significant amount of choice when adopting design-based assistance. This is consistent with NAS's conviction that educational change cannot be mandated "from above." Because of this belief, the designs require a significant majority buy-in on the part of school staff (e.g., 75 to 80 percent) before implementation can begin.

Engaging District Support

Initially, the NAS strategy focused primarily on schools. NAS believed that a national reform effort would be established if schools were transformed with the help of designs—one at a time. But this NAS strategy has evolved:

> Over the past four years, we have recognized that the power of school-by-school improvement is limited. The major evolution in the New American Schools strategy has been the growing convic-

---

evaluation attention and resources on key aspects of the program; (2) it facilitates aggregation of evaluation results into a broader base of theoretical and program knowledge; (3) it asks program practitioners to make their assumptions explicit and to reach consensus with their colleagues about what they are attempting to do and why; and (4) research and evaluation that address the theoretical assumptions embedded in programs may have more influence on both policy and popular opinion than do those that fail to address them.

tion that, without changes in the structure, policies, and practices of school systems, good schools will remain the exception (New American Schools Development Corporation, 1997, p. 5).

Thus, rather than breaking the molds of existing schools—one at a time—with fundamentally different models of organization, NAS aimed toward a "bottom-up, top-down" perspective that attempts to assist (1) districts to establish a conducive operating environment for the designs, and (2) schools to change their organization, professional development, standards, curriculum, and instruction to improve student learning.

NAS believes that the designs and the assistance they provide are likely to be widely successful only if they operate in jurisdictions that provide supportive environments. In such environments, school districts support design implementation in a number of ways (see Bodilly and Berends, 1999). For instance, before implementation, districts can encourage schools to assess their needs so that they can ask probing questions of the design teams about how those needs can best be met within the context of a schoolwide design. Such a process, among others, can further the appropriate match of the designs to schools based on district accountability demands, design capabilities, and school needs. Moreover, in supportive operating environments, there is a reasonably intense focus on design implementation for a limited number of years (e.g., three years). There are also adequate resources for accomplishing that implementation—a critical aspect that requires district leadership and stability (see Bodilly, 1998; Keltner, 1998). Such an approach assumes that this district focus on schoolwide transformation will lead to district policies that conform to and reinforce consistent and coherent strategies for school change. These include not only resource allocation, but policies related to hiring, curriculum, instruction, standards, and assessments as well.

In 1995, at the beginning of the scale-up phase, NAS partnered with ten jurisdictions: Cincinnati, Dade County, Kentucky, Maryland, Memphis, Philadelphia, Pittsburgh, San Antonio, San Diego, and Washington State.[4] The goal in each jurisdiction was to transform 30

---

[4]The districts in Kentucky, Pittsburgh, and San Diego were partners with the NARE design team. NARE was also active in Washington State.

percent of the schools within a five-year period using NAS or other schoolwide designs. While chosen arbitrarily, the 30 percent goal reflected the desire to ensure that design-based schools would form a critical mass within each jurisdiction.

RAND'S ASSESSMENT

The NAS approach relies on school designs and design-based assistance and requires the alignment of numerous institutional, social, political, and economic factors for successful implementation, consistency and coherence, and ultimate success. It is both ambitious and complex.[5] As a result, any assessment of the NAS initiative has to be multidimensional and multifaceted and must rely on a variety of data and a wide array of indicators. Such an assessment is a difficult and analytically complex undertaking. Yet it is critical to understanding the progress of schools implementing schoolwide reform, especially since so little research has been conducted in this relatively new educational policy area (see Herman, 1999; Fashola and Slavin, 1998; Pogrow, 1998).

To monitor the progress of the NAS initiative, RAND is addressing the five key questions outlined in Chapter One. These focus on issues related to the types of schools NAS design teams are assisting, the development of the design teams over time, changes in classroom environments in design-based schools and their effects on student achievement, and the implementation and performance trends in the NAS schools.

Data Collection Efforts

To address the issues of concern, RAND has used district-provided data and has undertaken a variety of data collection efforts: interviews, focus groups, case studies, surveys, observations, gathering of school and classroom artifacts, and document analysis. In a supplementary study of changes in classroom practice in an urban school district, we are administering a commercial test to a sample of fourth graders in NAS and non-NAS schools. All of these data inform

---

[5]For further discussions of this complexity, see Bodily, 1998; Glennan, 1998; and Fuhrman and Ritter, 1998.

our understanding of the reform that NAS is attempting to accomplish in districts, schools, classrooms, and the academic lives of students across the United States.

Monitoring a Longitudinal Sample of NAS Schools. For a longitudinal sample of schools, RAND is gathering data from districts, schools, principals, and teachers. We began collecting data at the beginning of NAS's scale-up phase, and we currently plan to continue these efforts through the 1999–2000 school year. A variety of data will help us to monitor the trends in implementation and performance at the NAS sites:

- *Teacher surveys administered to all teachers in NAS schools.* These surveys cover such topics as a teacher's understanding of the design; human, material, strategic, and other support available for design implementation; levels of implementation of key design elements; classroom activities in a target class; attitudes and perceptions toward teaching; professional development experiences; teacher background information; teacher's overall support for the design; satisfaction with student progress; and perceived effects of the design on the teacher's professional life and on student achievement and engagement.

- *Principal phone interviews.* These interviews, which take about an hour to complete, ask principals a series of closed and open-ended questions similar to those on the teacher survey. In addition, we ask principals about the aids and impediments to reform, the alignment between jurisdiction-sponsored tests and teaching and learning, teachers' professional development experiences, and school organizational characteristics.

- *District data on school performance indicators.* These include mandated test scores, attendance rates, promotion and dropout rates, and school demographic characteristics.

- *Site visits to schools and school districts.* The purpose of these site visits is to obtain district, school administrator, and teacher reports of the progress of the NAS initiative. One set of site visits is aimed particularly at schools and school districts no longer implementing NAS designs, the objective being to understand what led to the decision to stop. Another set focuses on particularly successful schools in order to understand what factors lead to success.

Monitoring Changes in Classroom Practices in San Antonio. In the spring of 1997, RAND began collecting data in selected NAS and non-NAS schools in San Antonio, Texas. This effort was to span two school years, ending in the spring of 1999.

For about 60 elementary classrooms, our task was to gather a wide variety of data over two school years:

- *Survey data from teachers.* These data include information on instructional practices, implementation of the designs, professional development, parental involvement, judgments about the effects of the design and support, and background characteristics.

- *Student-level data.* These data, gathered for all students in the elementary classrooms, include

    — Student background (gender, race-ethnicity, age, at-risk status, poverty, English proficiency, and prior test scores).

    — Test data from the Texas Assessment of Academic Skills (TAAS), which provides significant indicators for the state and district accountability systems.

    — Test data from the Stanford Achievement Open Ended Reading Test, Version 9 (SAT-9), which is a supplementary commercial test that asks students not only to read a passage and answer questions, but to explain their answers as well.

- *Principal phone interviews.* These interviews gather the same information gathered from the larger longitudinal sample of schools (see above).

- *More-specific data from classrooms.* For a subsample of about 15 teachers from the 60 classrooms, we are to collect additional data on instructional practices, such as

    — Observations of each teacher several times over the course of the school year.

    — Illustrative samples of students' work.

    — Teacher interviews and logs about assignments, homework, projects, quizzes and tests, and papers or reports over the course of the year.

In summary, we are gathering a wide array of data from districts, schools, design teams, principals, teachers, and students. We believe such a comprehensive data collection effort is needed to monitor and assess the progress of a reform effort as complex and varied as the NAS initiative.

Analytic Approach to Key Questions

We now return to the key questions of the RAND assessment of NAS and highlight our analytic approach to each of them. Table 2.1 summarizes the questions and our data collection activities. (Instruments and protocols for these studies are available from RAND upon request.)

What Were the NAS Schools Like Before They Implemented the Designs? This question is the focus of this report, which is the first in a series of reports based on analyses of the longitudinal sample RAND is using to monitor trends in implementation and performance. Most of the information in this report is based on data gathered before the NAS designs were implemented. As such, the report is a "baseline." With data provided by districts, we describe what the NAS schools were like (e.g., in terms of school performance, poverty, and racial-ethnic composition) before the designs began implementing and assisting. Moreover, we have retrospective survey data from principals to describe what their school climates were like early on in the scale-up phase.

How Have the Designs and the Assistance They Provide Evolved over Time? Since 1992, the designs and their teams have changed for many different reasons. We are examining the evolution of the designs based on document review and interviews over several years. This analysis addresses the question: What changes have been made to the designs and why? It will provide crucial information on the designs, the variation in foci among them, and the changes they made over time as they encountered implementation realities in schools facing significant challenges in terms of accountability systems, low test scores, poverty, diverse student populations, and difficult school climates.

Table 2.1

Key Questions of RAND Assessment and Data Collection Activities

	Teacher Surveys	Principal Phone Interviews	District Data on Schools	Site Visits	Focus Groups	Classroom Observations	Student Work Samples	Interviews	Document Review	Student Test Data and Background Information
What were the NAS schools like before they implemented the designs?		✓	✓							
How have the designs and the assistance they provide evolved over time?								✓	✓	
Are the critical components of the NAS designs being implemented across a wide array of schools? Why or why not?	✓	✓	✓	✓	✓			✓		
Do the NAS designs extend beyond changes in school organization and governance and permeate classrooms to change curriculum and instruction?	✓	✓	✓	✓	✓	✓	✓	✓	✓	✓
Over time, what is the progress of the schools being assisted by NAS design teams in improving student and school performance?	✓	✓	✓	✓	✓	✓	✓	✓	✓	✓

Are the Critical Components of the NAS Designs Being Implemented Across a Wide Array of Schools? Why or Why Not? As noted, we have collected two years' worth of data on teacher-reported design implementation levels and on principals' and teachers' views of this effort. These quantitative data will be complemented by interviews with district personnel to better understand how changes in district policies are related to and affect design implementation in schools.

To address this question, we will analyze

- Changes in implementation indicators, support for the designs, and teachers' judgments about the effects of the designs in their schools. We will use our teacher and principal survey data from the 1996–1997 and 1997–1998 school years and information provided through interviews of key decisionmakers in the different jurisdictions. Our indicators measure implementation in various areas: organization and governance, teacher professional life, instructional strategies and performance expectations, and involvement of parents and community.

- Insights from the jurisdiction interviews. Our objective is to understand the decision in some jurisdictions to stop implementing the designs and the importance to this decision of factors such as level and type of district support, new mandates, and teacher support.

- Differences among teachers, both within and among schools, related to variations in design implementation. The goal is to know more about how the implementation of a NAS design becomes a schoolwide reform effort. As designs continue to provide assistance and as teachers continue to become more familiar with the design team activities in their schools, we expect increases in implementation levels and agreement among teachers within schools.

Do the NAS Designs Extend Beyond Changes in School Organization and Governance and Permeate Classrooms to Change Curriculum and Instruction? A principal hypothesis of the NAS initiative is that schoolwide reform will be successful when design teams provide assistance to schools to fully implement the key design components.

A critical aim of this schoolwide reform is to improve classroom instruction and thereby improve student achievement and engagement.

This question focuses on changes in classroom practices. To answer it, RAND is conducting a supplementary study of classrooms in San Antonio to better understand the differences in instructional practices between NAS and non-NAS classrooms.

As part of this study, we are gathering a rich array of classroom-level data through observations, teacher interviews and focus groups, classroom artifacts, and teacher surveys. Such information will help provide answers to the question, Do NAS teachers and students interact with each other and with subject materials in ways that reflect the design teams' curricular and instructional theories of change? Our analyses and reporting of these data will include descriptive results about whether instructional practices promoted by the designs are occurring in NAS classrooms and will compare these practices to those in non-NAS classrooms.

Whether design-promoted instructional practices are related to student learning is clearly an important issue, and the data we collect in this effort will help us to address it. We describe the analyses related to the relationships among design implementation, instructional practices, and student achievement below.

Over Time, What Is the Progress of the Schools Being Assisted by NAS Design Teams in Improving Student and School Performance? Because the main goal of NAS and the design teams is to improve student learning, this is a crucial question in our assessment of the NAS initiative. However, as stated earlier, a variety of institutional, social, political, and economic factors must be aligned if implementation is to be successful and school performance improved. To address this question, our assessment draws on a variety of data, indicators, and analyses. Melding these together is a difficult and analytically complex undertaking. Even so, understanding the progress of schools implementing schoolwide reform is important, particularly in today's educational policy environment.

Our analyses informing this question include the following:

- For eight jurisdictions, we will analyze changes in performance outcomes between 1994–1995 (base year) and 1997–1998. That is, we will examine the progress of NAS schools in our sample over three years of implementation during the scale-up phase.

- We will use a wide array of data to help explain these implementation and performance trends. For example, we will link implementation measures to school performance indicators. In addition, interview and focus group information from case studies will provide a rich description of what has happened in these schools. That is, not only will we monitor the performance trends in a large sample of NAS schools, we will also provide explanations for why those trends occurred.

- We will use the San Antonio classroom data to examine the relationships among implementation, classroom instruction, and student achievement. We will examine the relationships between student achievement and a variety of individual and social factors, including (1) student characteristics (gender, race-ethnicity, at-risk status, age, English proficiency); (2) students' prior achievement (i.e., third-grade mathematics and reading scores); (3) classroom instruction; (4) design team activities; and (5) teacher background characteristics (education level, experience, age, gender, and race-ethnicity). To more accurately capture changes in student performance, we will have to assess the changes in student composition problems, as well as the mobility of teachers in our sample.

- As part of the San Antonio study, we will track the test scores of a fourth-grade cohort. We will be able to obtain scores for the fourth graders in our spring 1998 sample, as well as their third-grade (1997) and fifth-grade (1999) scores. So, over the course of this study, we will be able track scores for this year's cohort from grade 3 through grade 5. We will compare the trends of these NAS students to the trends of their non-NAS counterparts.

- Because our previous work indicates that school-level differences contribute significantly to the observed variation in implementation (Bodily, 1998), we intend in the spring of 2000 to explore this issue further by visiting schools that claim to be implementing the designs. On the basis of previous analyses of the longitudinal school sample described above, we will classify implementing schools as having produced low or high performance outcomes. Differences among these two groups will be explored to provide additional information about why performance differs in schools implementing NAS designs.

Our analyses of student performance would benefit greatly from the inclusion of individual-level test score data directly comparable across all implementing sites. However, participating districts were unwilling to consider additional testing because of the burden on schools, teachers, and students. Moreover, the cost of such testing could not be accommodated within the available funding. Thus, only in the study of classroom instruction is it feasible to administer a supplemental commercial test. While specialized tests, better matched to the design objectives, might have provided relevant information on the effects of the designs, the public expects performance to be measured against local accountability measures, which are what our analyses are based on.

We fully realize the problems inherent in attempting to identify a "design team" effect independent of the efforts of other curricular and instructional programs being implemented in NAS schools. Nonetheless, the combined analyses will provide important insights into levels of implementation, extent of assistance as reported by teachers, professional development, and the usefulness of the designs and design-based assistance for creating positive classroom and school environments that improve student learning.

SIGNIFICANT FEATURES OF RAND RESEARCH

The RAND assessment outlined above has a number of significant qualities designed to capture the complex nature of the NAS reform:

- It keeps a constant focus on implementation, using various methods to determine whether designs can be implemented in real schools facing significant challenges and whether the process for helping schools to choose among designs is effective.

- It recognizes that school transformation and performance are the joint products of a number of important factors: the design itself, the assistance provided by the design team, the environment for implementation provided by the school district, and the readiness of the school. While it cannot possibly isolate these factors completely from each other, the evaluation tries to provide some understanding of the contribution of each.

- Its design emphasizes school improvement over time. Rarely have data been gathered on a similar set of schools over time to monitor the progress of implementation and other crucial organizational and performance factors. Within RAND's longitudinal sample of NAS sites, schools serve as their own "controls." Over time, we examine whether each school's test scores improve, and we compare changes in school test scores to changes in district test scores. The reason we have not chosen to try more-complex quasi-experimental evaluation designs is that they most likely could not be effectively implemented, because of NAS's overall scale-up strategy.

- Its design reflects an understanding that school-centered reform requires substantial time. Our assessment spans a five-year period.

In summary, RAND's research on NAS strives to be a comprehensive assessment that will not only inform NAS, the design teams, and the partnering jurisdictions, but will also provide important lessons for those interested in comprehensive school reform.

Chapter Three

BASELINE DESCRIPTION OF
NEW AMERICAN SCHOOLS

In this chapter, we provide a baseline description for the NAS schools in our sample by addressing the following question: What were the demographic, climate, and performance characteristics of the schools that design teams began assisting at the beginning of scale-up? The unit of analysis here is the school; our aim is to understand what the characteristics of NAS schools were before the designs partnered with them.

We first discuss the sample of schools used for the descriptive results. We then describe the NAS schools in terms of their demographic characteristics—i.e., proportion of school in poverty and proportion of students from racial-ethnic minority backgrounds. We also discuss these schools' climate characteristics and compare them to a national sample. Finally, we summarize the schools' performance levels before the designs began implementation by presenting the baseline performance data provided by district data records.

SAMPLE OF NEW AMERICAN SCHOOLS

The sample consists of those schools initiating implementation of NAS designs in either the 1995–1996 or the 1996–1997 school year in eight jurisdictions:[1]

---

[1]When we decided on the longitudinal sample of schools, Maryland and San Diego were not far enough along in their implementation to warrant inclusion in our

- Cincinnati

- Dade County

- Kentucky

- Memphis

- Philadelphia

- Pittsburgh

- San Antonio

- Washington State

Our choice of jurisdictions reflected both our desire to obtain a sample that included all the designs participating in the scale-up phase and our judgment that the costs of working in the additional jurisdictions would not yield commensurate benefits. While jurisdictions and their support of the NAS reform will no doubt continue to change over time, the jurisdictions we chose reflect a range of support for implementation—from a great deal to very little (see Bodilly, 1998).

Our aim was to have a "census" sample of NAS schools within the jurisdictions selected.[2] That is, we wanted to gather information from all the principals and teachers at these sites. Based on our conversations with NAS in the late summer and early fall of 1996, we found that there were 256 schools implementing NAS designs across these eight jurisdictions. However, after further conversations with design teams, jurisdictions, and the schools, the sample was reduced to 184 for several reasons:

---

planned data collection efforts. Since then, several of the design teams report that they are implementing in Maryland and San Diego.

[2]It is important to note that our sample of NAS sites is drawn from a set of NAS schools that expressed interest in implementing designs in districts that had formed a partnership with NAS. While this may imply some bias, it is difficult to know which way the bias goes in all instances, because both the degree of free choice that schools had and the degree to which jurisdictions supported the NAS initiative varied (see Bodilly, 1998; Bodilly and Berends, 1999).

- Fifty-one RW schools in Dade County were low-performing and on the verge of serious sanctions by the state, so the district promised them that they would not be burdened with research.

- Another 21 schools declined to participate because they did not want to be burdened with research, were not implementing, or had dropped the design.

Table 3.1 breaks down the 184 schools in the longitudinal sample by jurisdiction.

SOURCES OF DATA

Data for the analyses reported here are drawn from publicly reported district data on school demographics (e.g., poverty and racial-ethnic composition) and test scores. In addition, we conducted phone interviews with school principals in the spring of 1997 to gather retrospective data on school climate characteristics. These interviews each took about one hour to complete.

RESPONSE RATES

The principals of 170 of the 184 schools (92 percent) responded to our phone interviews in the spring of 1997. The attained sample of 170 principal responses is shown by district and design in Table 3.2. We rely on these responses for the descriptions provided next.

Table 3.1

1995–1996 Target Sample for RAND Longitudinal Sample

Jurisdiction	AC	ATLAS	CON	ELOB	MR	NARE	RW	Total
Cincinnati			5	5			6	16
Dade County	5		4	1	3		4	17
Kentucky						51		51
Memphis	5	5	5	5	4		9	33
Philadelphia		12	4		2			18
Pittsburgh						12		12
San Antonio				8	5			13
Washington State		8				16		24
Total	10	25	18	19	14	79	19	184

Table 3.2

Principal Interview Sample, Spring 1997

Jurisdiction	AC	ATLAS	CON	ELOB	MR	NARE	RW	Total
Cincinnati			5	5			6	16
Dade County	5		4	1	3		4	17
Kentucky						44		44
Memphis	5	5	5	5	4		9	33
Philadelphia		9	2		2			13
Pittsburgh						10		10
San Antonio				8	5			13
Washington State		8				16		24
Total	10	22	16	19	14	70	19	170

DEMOGRAPHIC CHARACTERISTICS OF SCHOOLS

Most of the schools receiving design team assistance could be considered socially and academically disadvantaged in terms of poverty, racial-ethnic composition, climate, and student test scores. The NAS sites in our sample are below "average" when a number of school characteristics are compared to national norms.

About one-third of the nation's students receive free and reduced-price lunches.[3] On average, 55 percent of the students in each of the NAS schools in our sample can be categorized as being poor.

Figure 3.1 reveals that most of the design teams are assisting schools in partnering jurisdictions with high concentrations of poor stu-

---

[3]We measure school poverty as the percentage of students within a school who receive free and/or reduced-price lunches. Because all students in the San Antonio Independent School District receive free lunches, poverty there is measured as students within a school who are *eligible* for free and/or reduced-price lunches. In Philadelphia, free/reduced-price lunch information is not available, so the percentage of students receiving Aid to Families with Dependent Children (AFDC) benefits is used in its place. Reduced-price lunches and AFDC are both indicators used for allocation of federal Title I funding under the 1994 Improving America's Schools Act (see American Association of School Administrators, 1995; http://www.ed.gov/legislation/ESEA). Currently, schools can use their Title I funding for schoolwide improvement if at least 50 percent of the students within the school are from poor families (see U.S. Department of Education, 1993; Borman et al., 1996). The national averages for both school poverty and minority composition are based on the nationally representative Schools and Staffing Survey (SASS) of 1993–1994 (for a further description of these SASS data, see U.S. Department of Education, 1996).

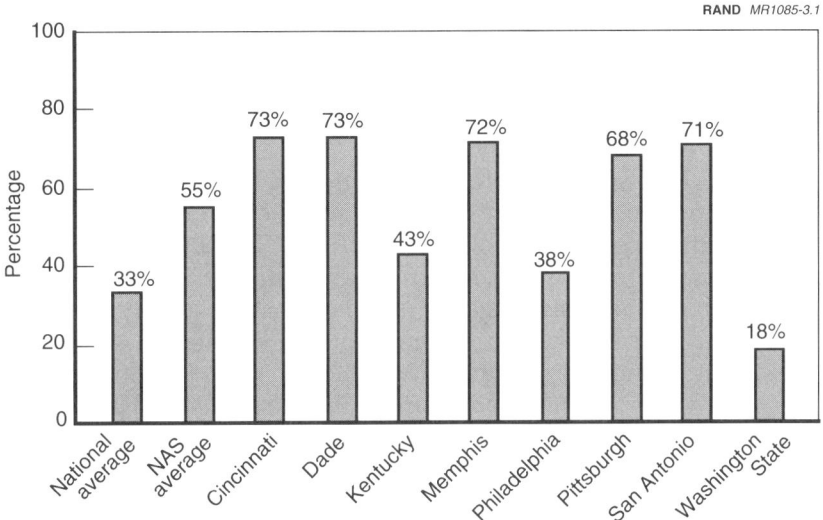

Figure 3.1—Percentage of Poor Students in NAS Schools, 1994–1995

dents. For example, the NAS schools in Cincinnati, Dade County, Memphis, Pittsburgh, and San Antonio are serving mostly poor student populations—i.e., over two-thirds of the students receive free or reduced-price lunches at these NAS sites. The percentage of poor in our Philadelphia jurisdiction is based on a more stringent measure of poverty: percentage of students receiving AFDC benefits. Thirty-eight percent of the students in the Philadelphia NAS schools are receiving AFDC benefits, reflecting the high poverty levels in this large, urban district.

The design team in Kentucky, NARE, assisted schools similar to those in the nation in terms of the percentage of students classified as poor. In Washington State, the design teams, ATLAS and NARE, are assisting schools that are more affluent than the national average. In fact, if the more affluent schools in the states of Kentucky and Washington are excluded, the school poverty composition of the NAS sample increases to 68 percent.

We also examined the racial-ethnic compositions of the NAS schools and compared them to the national average. While having a greater proportion of minority students in a school may be advantageous for students in some respects, a disproportionate number of minority students may also indicate problems associated with segregation and racial-ethnic isolation in the nation's schools (see Orfield and Eaton, 1996; Armor, 1995; Wells, 1995; Crain and Mahard, 1982).

About 35 percent of the nation's students are categorized as racial-ethnic minorities (see Figure 3.2). In contrast, on average, 57 percent of the students in NAS schools are minorities. The NAS design teams in Cincinnati, Dade County, Memphis, and San Antonio are assisting schools that have a vast majority of minority students. By contrast, the NAS schools in the states of Kentucky and Washington are mostly nonminority (non-Hispanic white) schools. If the Kentucky and Washington schools are removed from the sample, over 80 percent of the students in NAS schools are minorities. Thus, most of the NAS designs are assisting schools with disproportionately high percentages of racial-ethnic minority students.

In short, whether considering school poverty or racial-ethnic composition, most of the NAS sites are not reflective of the nation. In

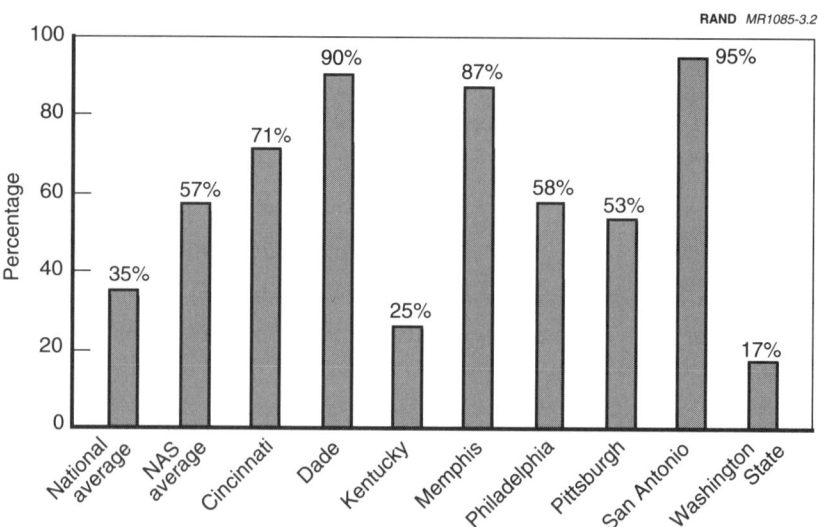

Figure 3.2—Percentage of Racial-Ethnic Minority Students in NAS Schools, 1994–1995

fact, these indicators suggest the NAS designs are assisting mostly urban schools facing significant challenges related to school poverty and racial-ethnic segregation.

SCHOOL CLIMATE: NAS SCHOOLS COMPARED TO THE NATION'S SCHOOLS

How do the school climates in the NAS sites compare to those of U.S. schools generally? In our spring of 1997 phone interviews, we asked principals several questions about school climate. Specifically, we asked them to provide retrospective reports about the severity of various problems in their schools. The questions were taken from a national survey so that we could compare the NAS principal responses to those of a nationally representative sample of principals.[4] We compared NAS principals to the nation's principals along two sets of school problems related to

1. Diverse student populations, as indicated by principal reports of the severity of school problems connected with

    - poverty

    - difficulties with the English language

    - racial tension

    - lack of school readiness[5]

2. Engagement, as indicated by

    - student absenteeism

    - teacher absenteeism

    - verbal abuse of teachers

    - student disrespect of teachers

---

[4]We compared our NAS results to the nationally representative SASS of 1993–1994. (For a further description of these SASS data, see U.S. Department of Education, 1996.)

[5]For the sake of parsimony, we created a composite for *school readiness*, a scale including principals' reports of problems with student apathy, lack of academic challenge, students coming unprepared to learn, poor nutrition, and poor health. The alpha reliability of this scale was .80 in the NAS data and .83 in the SASS data.

In the figures that follow, we present the percentage of principals at the NAS sites and in the nation who rated these problems as "moderate" or "serious." We report our results separately for elementary and secondary schools because the severity of several of these indicators differs across these levels.

Problems Related to Diverse Student Populations

Compared to a national sample of principals, a greater percentage of NAS principals report problems related to poverty, difficulties with the English language, racial tension, and school readiness (see Figures 3.3 and 3.4). For example, almost two-thirds of NAS elementary and secondary principals report moderate to serious problems related to the level of student poverty in their schools. Less than 50 percent of the nation's principals report such problems.

In both elementary and secondary schools, there is a difference between the NAS sites and the national sample of about five to eight

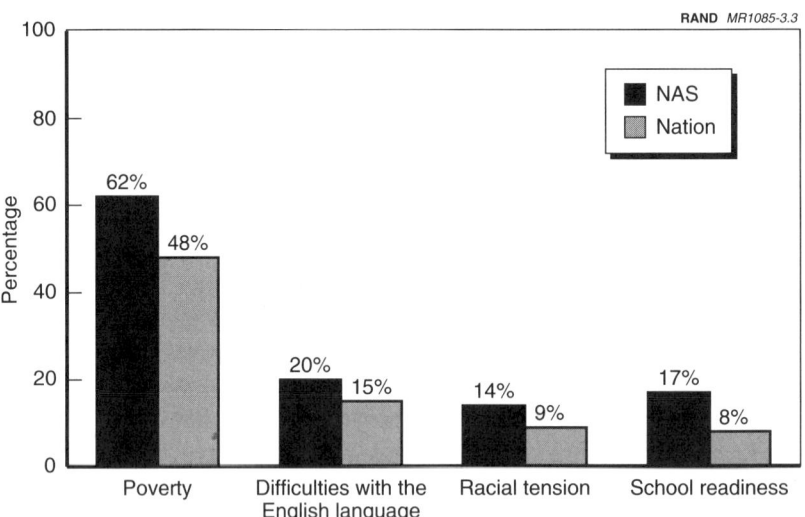

Figure 3.3—Percentage of Elementary School Principals
Reporting Moderate to Serious Problems Related to
Diverse Student Populations

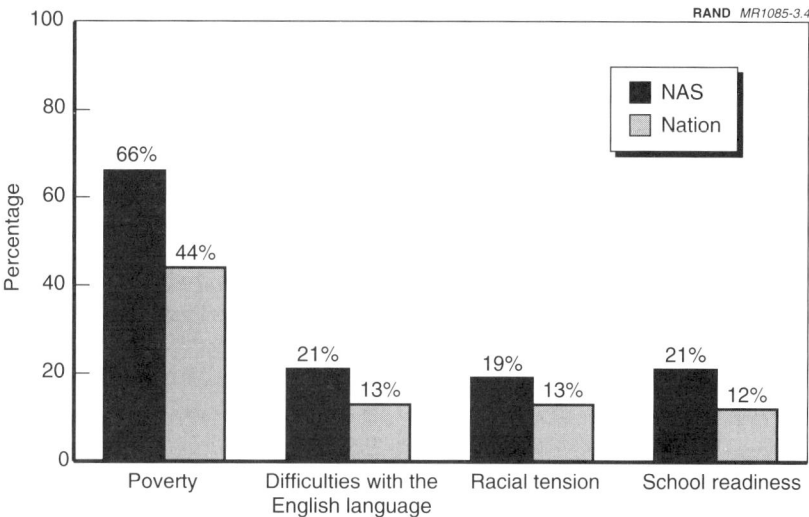

Figure 3.4—Percentage of Secondary School Principals
Reporting Moderate to Serious Problems Related to
Diverse Student Populations

percentage points when considering difficulties with the English language and racial tension.

There is a more marked difference between NAS schools and the nation with respect to school readiness. In fact, the severity of the school readiness problems reported by the NAS elementary principals is roughly twice that reported by principals across the nation (17 vs. 8 percent). In secondary schools, 21 percent of the NAS principals report moderate to serious problems with school readiness, compared to 12 percent of the nation's principals.

Problems Related to Engagement of Students and Faculty

The NAS schools also presented challenges related to the engagement of students and teachers in the education process. Compared to the national sample of principals, a greater percentage of NAS principals report moderate to serious problems with student absenteeism, teacher absenteeism, verbal abuse of teachers by students, and student disrespect of teachers (see Figures 3.5 and 3.6). For example, over 40 percent of NAS elementary principals report problems with student absenteeism, compared to 20 percent of the nation's principals. In addition, while 11 percent of the nation's elementary school principals report problems with teachers being absent from work, 33 percent of NAS principals report teacher absenteeism problems.

In secondary schools, problems with student verbal abuse and disrespect of teachers are much greater in NAS schools than in the nation as a whole. For instance, about one-half of the NAS secondary school principals report moderate to serious problems with student disrespect of teachers, compared to about one-quarter of the nation's principals. Moreover, the percentage of NAS secondary school principals reporting problems with verbal abuse of teachers is more than twice that of the nation's principals reporting such problems (43 percent vs. 18 percent).

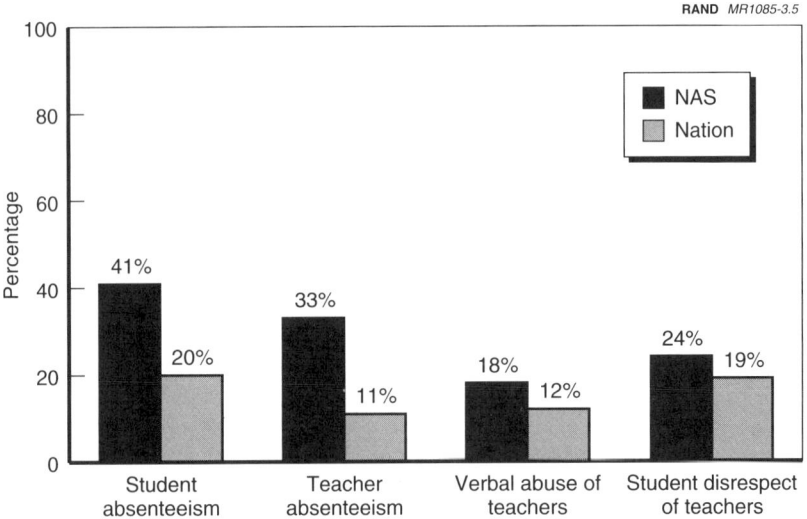

Figure 3.5—Percentage of Elementary School Principals Reporting
Moderate to Serious Problems Related to Engagement

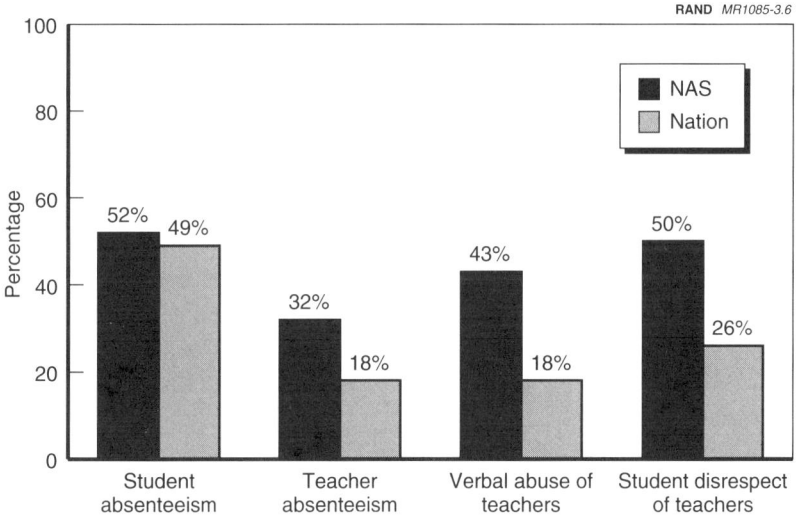

Figure 3.6—Percentage of Secondary School Principals Reporting
Moderate to Serious Problems Related to Engagement

SCHOOL ACHIEVEMENT BEFORE DESIGN IMPLEMENTATION

To understand the progress of NAS schools, particularly in terms of the schools' performance on achievement tests, requires an understanding of schools' achievement levels before designs were implemented.

In general, the NAS schools were in low-performing, urban school districts. Within these districts and with few exceptions, the NAS design teams began assisting schools that were scoring at or below the district average on district or state-mandated tests.

Rather than provide each comparison by grade level, jurisdiction, and test, we present, in Figure 3.7, a summary of the comparisons we made among grade levels and types of tests in the different districts. While the tests and the reporting of them to the public differ dramatically across the jurisdictions, our aim was to compare the NAS school scores to the district averages and categorize them as below (black in Figure 3.7), at (gray), or above (white) those averages.[6]

RAND MR1085-3.7

NAS schools in:	Reading (NAS sites compared to the entire district/state)			Mathematics (NAS sites compared to the entire district/state)		
	Elementary	Middle	High	Elementary	Middle	High
Cincinnati (CAT) Grades 5 & 7			Not applicable			Not applicable
Dade (SAT-8) Grades 4, 8, & 11						
Kentucky (KIRIS) Grades 4, 8, & 12						
Memphis (CTBS) Grades 4, 8, & 10						
Philadelphia (SAT-9) Grades 4, 8, & 11						Not applicable
Pittsburgh (ITBS, TAP) Grades 1–5, 6–8, & 9						
San Antonio (TAAS) Grades 4, 8, & 10						
Washington (CTBS) Grades 4 & 8			Not applicable			Not applicable

CAT: California Achievement Test
CTBS: Comprehensive Test of Basic Skills
ITBS: Iowa Test of Basic Skills
KIRIS: Kentucky Instructional Results Information System
SAT-8: Stanford Achievement Test, Version 8
SAT-9: Stanford Achievement Test, Version 9
TAAS: Texas Assessment of Academic Skills
TAP: Test of Achievement and Proficiency

Lower ←——————→ Higher

Figure 3.7—Baseline Achievement Levels of NAS Sites Compared to District or State Averages on Standardized Tests

---

[6]We classified schools as above or below the district average if they were plus or minus (1) .2 of a standard deviation on the grade-level test scores and we had access to student-level test score data (i.e., Kentucky), (2) 5 percentage points if scores were reported as average percentile scores, or (3) 7 percentage points if scores were reported as median percentile scores. These cut-points are somewhat arbitrary. For example, Fashola and Slavin (1998) suggest using somewhat more stringent criteria (e.g., effect size of .25 of a standard deviation). Nonetheless, we believe that the criteria above suffice for the basic point that even within low-performing districts, the NAS design teams began assisting schools that were at or below the district average.

In general, the NAS schools were scoring at or below the district test score averages before the NAS designs began assisting them, even in jurisdictions that are primarily low-performing compared to state averages. The NAS sites in Washington State are the exception because they tend to be more affluent, as indicated by the percentage of students eligible for free and/or reduced-price lunches.

Chapter Four

SUMMARY OF FINDINGS AND WORK AHEAD

The NAS designs are attempting to change the academic lives of students and the professional lives of teachers in difficult environments. The baseline information provided here shows clearly that the NAS design teams began assisting some very challenged schools when they started implementing the designs during NAS's scale-up phase. For the most part, NAS designs entered schools that were primarily urban, low-performing, poor, and minority.

The NAS schools also have more difficult climates than most of the nation's schools do. In comparing the NAS school climate indicators to a national sample, we find that NAS principals report greater problems related to diverse student populations—poverty, difficulty with the English language, racial tension, and school readiness. The schools in which the NAS designs were being implemented were also facing challenges associated with engaging students and teachers (as indicated by student and teacher absenteeism, student verbal abuse, and student disrespect of teachers).

The vast majority of the NAS schools are in low-performing, urban districts. For the most part, except in Washington State, the NAS designs entered schools that were performing at or below the district average on the mandated tests administered in each jurisdiction. In short, the NAS designs are not assisting a set of socially or academically advantaged schools. Rather, the schools being assisted are facing significant challenges.

Whether designs and the assistance they provide to these schools improve the educational opportunities and outcomes for the students is a crucial question. To address this question, our assessment, described in this report, is drawing on a variety of data, indicators, and analyses. Blending these together is a difficult and analytically complex undertaking. However, examining the relationships among implementation, school and student performance, and related social and organizational factors is critical for understanding comprehensive school reform and its promise for our nation's future.

REFERENCES

American Association of School Administrators (1995). *Great Expectations: Understanding the New Title I.* Washington, DC: American Association of School Administrators.

Armor, D. J. (1995). *Forced Justice: School Desegregation and the Law.* New York: Oxford University Press.

Ball, D. L., E. Camburn, D. K. Cohen, and B. Rowan (1998). "Instructional Improvement and Disadvantaged Students." Unpublished manuscript, University of Michigan.

Bodilly, S. J. (1996). *Lessons from New American Schools Development Corporation's Demonstration Phase.* Santa Monica, CA: RAND (MR-729-NASDC).

Bodilly, S. J. (1998). *Lessons from New American Schools' Scale-Up Phase: Prospects for Bringing Designs to Multiple Schools.* Santa Monica, CA: RAND (MR-1777-NAS).

Bodilly, S. J., and M. Berends (1999). "Necessary District Support for Comprehensive School Reform." In *Hard Work for Good Schools: Facts not Fads in Title I Reform*, edited by G. Orfield and E. H. DeBray. Boston, MA: Harvard Civil Rights Project.

Bodilly, S. J., S. Purnell, K. Ramsey, and C. Smith (1995). *Designing New American Schools: Baseline Observations on Nine Design Teams.* Santa Monica, CA: RAND (MR-598-NASDC).

Borman, K. M., P. W. Cookson, Jr., A. R. Sadovnik, and J. Z. Spade (1996). (Editors). *Implementing Educational Reform: Sociological*

Perspectives on Educational Policy. Norwood, NJ: Ablex Publishing Corporation.

Bryk, A. S., P. B. Sebring, D. Kerbow, S. Rollow, and J. Q. Easton (1998). *Charting Chicago School Reform: Democratic Localism as a Lever for Change.* Boulder, CO: Westview.

Crain, R. L., and R. E. Mahard (1982). *Desegregation Plans that Raise Black Achievement: A Review of the Research.* Santa Monica, CA: RAND (N-1844-NIE).

Cuban, L. (1990). "Reforming Again, Again, and Again." *Educational Researcher,* 19(1), pp. 3–13.

Datnow, A., and S. Stringfield (1997). *School Effectiveness and School Improvement,* 8(1).

Fashola, O. S., and R. E. Slavin (1998). "Schoolwide Reform Models: What Works?" *Phi Delta Kappan,* 79(5), pp. 370–379.

Furhman, S. H., and G. W. Ritter (1998). "External School Reform Providers and Accountability." Unpublished manuscript, Graduate School of Education, University of Pennsylvania.

Gamoran, A., and M. Berends (1987). "The Effects of Stratification in Secondary Schools: Synthesis of Survey and Ethnographic Research." *Review of Educational Research,* 57, pp. 415–435.

Gamoran, A., M. Nystrand, M. Berends, and P. C. LePore (1995). "An Organizational Analysis of the Effects of Ability Grouping." *American Educational Research Journal,* 32, pp. 687–715.

Glennan, T. K., Jr. (1998). *New American Schools After Six Years.* Santa Monica, CA: RAND (MR-945-NASDC).

Hallinan, M. T. (1994). "Tracking: From Theory to Practice." *Sociology of Education,* 67(2), pp. 79–83.

Herman, R. (1999). *An Educators' Guide to Schoolwide Reform.* Arlington, VA: Educational Research Service.

Jencks, C., and P. E. Peterson (1991). (Editors). *The Urban Underclass.* Washington, DC: The Brookings Institution.

Jencks, C., and M. Phillips (1998). (Editors). *The Black-White Test Score Gap*. Washington, DC: The Brookings Institution Press.

Johnson, J., and J. Immerwahr (1994). *First Things First: What Americans Expect from the Public Schools*. New York: Public Agenda.

Keltner, B. (1998). *Resources for Transforming New American Schools: First Year Findings*. Santa Monica: RAND (IP-175).

Kliebard, H. M. (1986). *The Struggle for the American Curriculum 1893–1958*. Boston, MA: Routledge and Kegan Paul.

Kozol, J. (1991). *Savage Inequalities: Children in America's Schools*. New York: Crown.

Lortie, D. (1970). *School Teacher*. Chicago, IL: University of Chicago Press.

Mitchell, K. (1996). *Reforming and Conforming: NASDC Principals Discuss School Accountability Systems*. Santa Monica, CA: RAND (MR-716-NASDC).

Murphy, J. (1991). *Restructuring Schools: Capturing and Assessing the Phenomena*. New York: Teachers College Press.

National Research Council (1997). *The New Americans: Economic, Demographic, and Fiscal Effects of Immigration*. Washington, DC: National Academy Press.

New American Schools Development Corporation (1997). *Bringing Success to Scale: Sharing the Vision of New American Schools*. Arlington, VA: New American Schools Development Corporation.

New American Schools Development Corporation (1999). "New American Schools: An Update to the Board of Directors." Unpublished presentation.

Newmann, F. M., and Associates (1996). (Editor). *Authentic Achievement: Restructuring Schools for Intellectual Quality*. San Francisco: Jossey Bass.

Oakes, J. (1994). "More Than Misapplied Technology: A Normative and Political Response to Hallinan on Tracking." *Sociology of Education*, 67(2), pp. 84–88.

Oakes, J., A. Gamoran, and R. N. Page (1992). "Curriculum Differentiation: Opportunities, Outcomes, and Meanings." In *Handbook of Research on Curriculum*, edited by P. W. Jackson. New York: Macmillan.

Orfield, G., and S. E. Eaton (1996). *Dismantling Desegregation: The Quiet Reversal of Brown v. Board of Education*. New York: The New Press.

Pogrow, S. (1998). "What Is an Exemplary Program, and Why Should Anyone Care? A Reaction to Slavin and Klein." *Educational Researcher*, 27(7), pp. 22–29.

Powell, A. G., E. Farrar, and D. K. Cohen (1985). *The Shopping Mall High School: Winners and Losers in the Educational Marketplace*. Boston: Houghton Mifflin.

Ross, S. M., W. L. Sanders, S. P. Wright, and S. Stringfield (1998). "The Memphis Restructuring Initiative: Achievement Results for Years 1 and 2 on the Tennessee Value-Added Assessment System (TVAAS)." Unpublished manuscript, University of Memphis.

Ross, S., A. Troutman, D. Horgan, S. Maxwell, R. Laitinen, and D. Lowther (1997). "The Success of Schools in Implementing Eight Restructuring Designs: A Synthesis of First Year Evaluation Outcomes." *School Effectiveness and School Improvement*, 8(1), pp. 95–124.

Sizer, T. R. (1984). *Horace's Compromise: The Dilemma of the American High School*. Boston: Houghton Mifflin.

Slavin, R. E. (1987). "Ability Grouping and Student Achievement in Elementary Schools: A Best-Evidence Synthesis." *Review of Educational Research*, 57, pp. 293–336.

Slavin, R. E. (1990). "Achievement Effects of Ability Grouping in Secondary Schools: A Best-Evidence Synthesis." *Review of Educational Research*, 60, pp. 471–499.

Smith, J. (1995). *Unequal Wealth and Incentives to Save*. Santa Monica: RAND (DB-145-RC).

Stringfield, S., and A. Datnow (1998). (Editors). *Education and Urban Society*, 30(3).

Stringfield, S., M. A. Millsap, and R. Herman (1997). *Special Strategies for Educating Disadvantaged Children: Findings and Policy Implications of a Longitudinal Study.* Washington, DC: U.S. Department of Education.

Stringfield, S., S. Ross, and L. Smith (1996). (Editors). *Bold Plans for School Restructuring: The New American Schools Designs.* Mahwah, NJ: Lawrence Erlbaum.

Sykes, G. (1990). "Fostering Teacher Professionalism in Schools." In *Restructuring Schools: The Next Generation of Educational Reform*, edited by R. F. Elmore. San Francisco: Jossey-Bass.

Tyack, D., and L. Cuban (1995). *Tinkering Toward Utopia: A Century of Public School Reform.* Cambridge, MA: Harvard University Press.

U.S. Department of Education (1993). *Improving America's Schools Act of 1993: The Reauthorization of the Elementary and Secondary Education Act and Other Amendments.* Washington, DC: U.S. Department of Education.

U.S. Department of Education (1996). *Schools and Staffing in the United States: A Statistical Profile, 1993–1994.* By R. R. Henke, S. P. Choy, S. Geis, and S. P. Groughman. Washington, DC: National Center for Education Statistics (NCES 96-124).

Weiss, C. H. (1972). *Evaluation Research: Methods for Assessing Program Effectiveness.* Englewood Cliffs, NJ: Prentice Hall.

Weiss, C. H. (1995). "Nothing as Practical as Good Theory: Exploring Theory-Based Evaluation for Comprehensive Community Initiatives for Children and Families." In *New Approaches to Evaluating Community Initiatives: Concepts, Methods, and Contexts*, edited by J. P. Connell, A. C. Kubisch, L. B. Schorr, and C. H. Weiss. Aspen, CO: The Aspen Institute, pp. 65–92.

Weiss, C. H. (1997). "How Can Theory-Based Evaluation Make Greater Headway?" *Evaluation Review*, 21(4), pp. 501–524.

Wells, A. S. (1995). "Reexamining Social Science Research on School Desegregation: Long- Versus Short-Term Effects." *Teachers College Record,* 96, pp. 691–706.

Wise, A. E. (1989). "Professional Teaching: A New Paradigm for the Management of Education." In *Schooling for Tomorrow: Directing Reforms to Issues That Count,* edited by T. J. Sergiovanni and J. H. Moore. Boston: Allyn and Bacon.